The Ultimate Guitar
SCALE CHART

Introduction

The *Ultimate Guitar Scale Chart* has been created to assist you in learning to play today's most commonly used scales. It is a fast and fun way to gain instant access to 120 scale patterns: just look up a scale and you can easily find out how and where to play it on the guitar.

This book will not only show you the different scales and their locations, it will provide the fundamentals behind *how* and *why* each scale is constructed. This will greatly enhance your playing and understanding of scales.

How to Use This Book

To use the scale chart on the following pages, simply find the root of the scale (C, D, E, etc.) in the column at the left, and the scale type (major, minor, etc.) along the top of the chart. Read down and across to find the correct chord. The fingerings are indicated with fingerboard diagrams, like this:

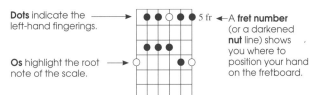

In general, when playing these scale patterns, keep your hand in one postion, and follow the "one-finger-per-fret" rule—that is, first finger on the 1st fret, second finger on the 2nd fret, and so on.

However, if a scale covers five or six frets, you will need to break this rule.
To play these patterns, you must either:

- stretch your hand to cover the wider distance, or
- shift your hand up (or down) the fingerboard.

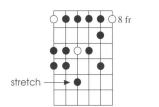
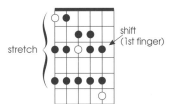
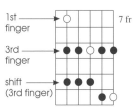

NOTE: All of the scale patterns in this book are *movable*—that is, they can be easily shifted up or down the fingerboard to accommodate any key or root note. Refer to the *guitar fingerboard chart* at right to find other locations of a scale or to better understand the component notes of a given fingering.

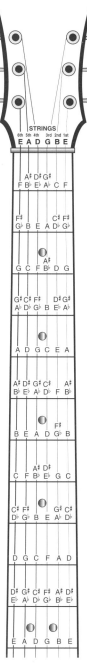

ISBN 0-634-01441-2

HAL•LEONARD®
CORPORATION
7777 W. BLUEMOUND RD. P.O. BOX 13819 MILWAUKEE, WI 53213

Visit Hal Leonard online at
www.halleonard.com

D1452316

	MAJOR	MINOR	MAJOR PENTATONIC	MINOR PENTATONIC	HARMONIC MINOR
C	7 fr	8 fr	5 fr	8 fr	8 fr
C♯/D♭	8 fr	9 fr	6 fr	9 fr	9 fr
D	5 fr	5 fr	5 fr	5 fr	5 fr
D♯/E♭	6 fr	6 fr	6 fr	6 fr	6 fr

	MELODIC MINOR	BLUES	MIXOLYDIAN	DORIAN	LYDIAN
C	5 fr	8 fr	5 fr	8 fr	7 fr
C♯/D♭	6 fr	9 fr	6 fr	9 fr	8 fr
D	5 fr	5 fr	5 fr	5 fr	5 fr
D♯/E♭	6 fr	6 fr	6 fr	6 fr	6 fr

	MAJOR	MINOR	MAJOR PENTATONIC	MINOR PENTATONIC	HARMONIC MINOR
E	7 fr	7 fr	7 fr	7 fr	7 fr
F					
F♯/G♭					
G		3 fr			3 fr

	MELODIC MINOR	BLUES	MIXOLYDIAN	DORIAN	LYDIAN
E					
F					
F♯/G♭					
G					

	MAJOR	MINOR	MAJOR PENTATONIC	MINOR PENTATONIC	HARMONIC MINOR
G♯/A♭	3 fr	4 fr	3 fr	4 fr	4 fr
A	4 fr	5 fr	4 fr	5 fr	5 fr
A♯/B♭	5 fr	6 fr	5 fr	6 fr	6 fr
B	6 fr	7 fr	6 fr	7 fr	7 fr

	MELODIC MINOR	BLUES	MIXOLYDIAN	DORIAN	LYDIAN
G♯/A♭	4 fr	4 fr	3 fr	4 fr	3 fr
A	5 fr	5 fr	4 fr	5 fr	4 fr
A♯/B♭	6 fr	6 fr	5 fr	6 fr	5 fr
B	7 fr	7 fr	6 fr	7 fr	6 fr

ABOUT SCALES

What Is a Scale?

A **scale** is a series of notes arranged in ascending or descending order. (The word "scale" comes from the Latin *scala*, which means "ladder.") Scales are important to know on the guitar, especially when creating riffs, licks, and solos.

How Are Scales Formed?

Scales are constructed using a combination of *whole steps* and *half steps*. (On the guitar, a *half step* is the distance of one fret; a *whole step* is two frets.) Perhaps the most common scale is the *major scale*, shown here in C:

C major scale

	whole step	whole step	half step	whole step	whole step	whole step	half step
	C	D	E	F	G	A	B	C
scale step:	1	2	3	4	5	6	7	8(1)

Notice the pattern above: *whole–whole–half–whole–whole–whole–half*. This is the "major scale" step pattern, which can be applied to any root note to create any major scale—C major, D major, E major, etc.

Notice also that each scale step above is numbered: 1-2-3-4-5-6-7. The chart to the right is a construction summary of the scale types in this book (based on the key of C only). Use the numeric formulas to determine the notes of a particular scale. For example, based on a C root, 1–2–♭3–4–5–♭6–♭7 would mean to play C–D–E♭–F–G–A♭–B♭—in other words, a C minor scale.

SCALE TYPE	FORMULA	NOTE NAMES
major	1-2-3-4-5-6-7	C-D-E-F-G-A-B
minor	1-2-♭3-4-5-♭6-♭7	C-D-E♭-F-G-A♭-B♭
major pentatonic	1-2-3-5-6	C-D-E-G-A
minor pentatonic	1-♭3-4-5-♭7	C-E♭-F-G-B♭
harmonic minor	1-2-♭3-4-5-♭6-7	C-D-E♭-F-G-A♭-B
melodic minor	1-2-♭3-4-5-6-7	C-D-E♭-F-G-A-B
blues	1-♭3-4-♭5-5-♭7	C-E♭-F-G♭-G-B♭
Mixolydian	1-2-3-4-5-6-♭7	C-D-E-F-G-A-B♭
Dorian	1-2-♭3-4-5-6-♭7	C-D-E♭-F-G-A-B♭
Lydian	1-2-3-♯4-5-6-7	C-D-E-F♯-G-A-B

How Are Scales Used?

Here are a few points to keep in mind when improvising with scales:

- You don't need to play scales from root to root; this is simply the way that they are best demonstrated. The notes of a scale can be played *in any order*, and you don't need to use them all. The root is often the most important note.

- Try to choose a scale that goes with the overall key of a song, or song section, not just with a single chord; this will allow you to improvise most effectively, using a single scale pattern.

- In general, when playing in a *major key*, try any of the following scales:
  major, major pentatonic, blues, Mixolydian, or **Lydian.**

  When playing in a *minor key*, try these:
  minor, minor pentatonic, harmonic minor, melodic minor, blues, or **Dorian.**